A NOTE TO PARENTS ABOUT BEING MEAN

In a recent study, 83% of the children interviewed reported that "being mean" is the worst thing one child can do to another. When asked to define "being mean," the children listed misbehaviors that included everything from "saying mean things" to "beating up on someone." When asked to name people who might be considered mean, "wicked stepmothers, monsters, and bad guys" were at the top of the list.

While it is not likely that your child will be mistreated by a wicked stepmother, monster, or bad guy, it is almost certain that he or she will be treated unkindly by a peer. When this happens, it is beneficial for your child to know how to respond appropriately. Fighting fire with fire—responding to unkind behavior by being unkind—is seldom productive. Behavior based on the Golden Rule (Treat others the way you want to be treated.) usually produces more satisfactory results.

This book teaches children about what prompts mean behavior. Knowing this can help children avoid personalizing another's misbehavior. It can also help children understand why they sometimes want to be mean and what they can do to resist these urges. When adults treat each other unkindly, they teach children to do the same. Living the Golden Rule is far more effective than preaching it.

This book belongs to:

Paaveli Douglau Horace

Published by Scholastic Inc.
90 Old Sherman Turnpike, Danbury, CT 06816.

SCHOLASTIC and associated logos are trademarks and/or
registered trademarks of Scholastic Inc.

ISBN 0-7172-8591-X

First Scholastic Printing, October 2005

A Book About
Being Mean

by
Joy Berry

SCHOLASTIC INC.

New York   Toronto   London   Auckland   Sydney
Mexico City   New Delhi   Hong Kong   Buenos Aires

This is Robbie and Katie. Reading about Robbie and Katie can help you understand why people are sometimes mean. It can also help you avoid being mean to others.

If you do something on purpose to hurt another person, you are being mean. When you are being mean to someone, you intentionally hurt the person's

- body,
- feelings, or
- belongings.

Sometimes people are mean because they want attention. They want to be noticed.

Being mean will not get you the kind of attention you want or need.

Try not to be mean when you need or want attention. Do these things instead:

- Tell someone in a kind way that you need attention.
- Ask the person to spend some time with you.

Sometimes people are mean because they don't know a better way to be funny. They want to make themselves or other people laugh.

Doing something that hurts someone or damages something is never funny. Being mean is never funny!

Try not to be mean when you want to be funny. Before you do something you think is funny to another person, be certain that

- the person will agree that what you are doing is funny,
- the person will not be hurt in any way, and
- no one's belongings will be damaged.

HE DOESN'T THINK THAT WHAT YOU DID IS FUNNY AND NEITHER DO I!
GULP!
SIGH
I'M GLAD I WASN'T IN THAT HAT!

Some people are mean because they feel angry or frustrated and don't know a better way to express their anger or frustration.

Being mean is not a good way to express anger or frustration. Being mean often creates situations that will make you feel even more angry or more frustrated.

Try not to express your anger or frustration by being mean. It is OK to express your anger or frustration by crying, yelling, jumping up and down, or hitting something that cannot be damaged (such as a pillow, punching bag, or bed). To avoid bothering anyone, you might need to go outside or into a room by yourself and close the door.

Some people are mean because they have been hurt and they want to get back at someone. These people try to make themselves feel better by

- hurting the person who has hurt them or
- hurting someone else.

Getting back at someone is not a good way to make yourself feel better when you are hurt. Getting back at someone might make the person want to get back at you, and you might get hurt again.

Try not to be mean when you have been hurt. Do these things instead:

- Talk to the person who has hurt you. Let the person know that you have been hurt and that you feel bad about whatever happened.
- Stay away from the person who has hurt you until you are certain that he or she will not hurt you again.

It is important to treat other people the way you want to be treated. If you don't want other people to be mean to you, you should not be mean to them.

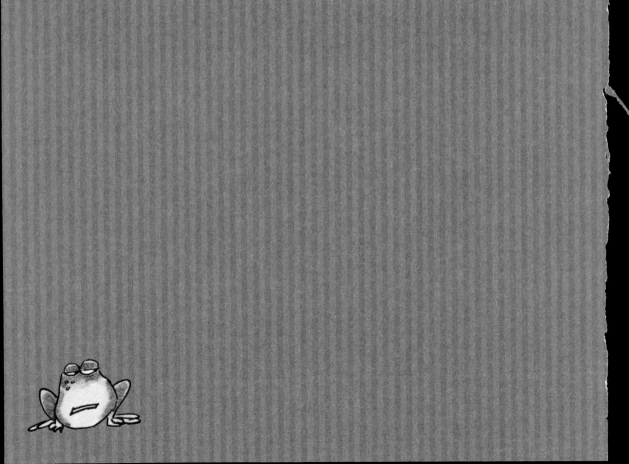